AFE 2983
23
18.00

D1503708

TEEN
HOT LINE

EATING DISORDERS

Charles Patterson

RSVP
RAINTREE
STECK-VAUGHN
PUBLISHERS
The Steck-Vaughn Company

Austin, Texas

Consultants:
Antonia Flint, MSW, ACSW, Psychotherapist, Trinity Counseling Service,
   Princeton, NJ
William B. Presnell, American Association for Marriage and Family Therapy

Developed for Steck-Vaughn Company by Visual Education Corporation, Princeton, New Jersey
Project Director: Paula McGuire
Editors: Jewel Moulthrop, Linda Perrin
Photo Research: Sara Matthews

Raintree Steck-Vaughn Publishers staff
Editor: Kathy Presnell
Project Manager: Julie Klaus
Electronic Production: Scott Melcer
Photo Editor: Margie Foster

Library of Congress Cataloging-in-Publication Data
Patterson, Charles.
   Eating disorders / Charles Patterson.
      p.   cm. — (Teen hot line)
   Includes index.
   ISBN 0-8114-3813-9
   1. Eating disorders in adolescence.   I. Title.   II. Series.
   RJ506.E18P38 1995
   616.85'26 — dc20   94-32116
                                                      CIP
                                                      AC

Photo Credits: Cover: © Michael Newman/PhotoEdit; **14:** © Michael Newman/PhotoEdit; **23:** The Bettmann Archive; **24:** © Merritt A. Vincent; **32:** © Kathy Sloane; **36:** Shirley Zeiberg; **42:** © Mary Kate Denny/PhotoEdit; **44:** © Michael Newman/PhotoEdit; **57:** © Richard Hutchings/PhotoEdit; **65:** © David Young-Wolff/PhotoEdit; **70:** © D&I MacDonald/Unicorn.

Printed and bound in the United States

2 3 4 5 6 7 8 9 0 LB 99 98 97 96

CONTENTS

What the
Teen
Hot Line
Is All About

This book is like a telephone hot line. It answers questions about eating disorders that may puzzle you. You can use that information to make your own decisions about what to do if you think you—or someone you know—has an eating disorder. Think of us as the voice on the phone, there to answer your questions, even the ones that are hard to ask.

To help you understand what eating disorders are all about, here is a list of steps we think you should take if you or someone you know has a serious eating problem. These steps focus on using common sense and finding out the facts. They assume that you want to make your own decisions and that you want to behave responsibly.

1 Find out everything you can about eating disorders by reading this and other books and talking to informed people. Ask your parents and friends to help you.

2 Remember that an eating disorder is not a permanent problem or a sign of a weak character. Someone who has an eating disorder needs help, just like someone who is physically ill. With care, he or she can recover from it.

3 Remember that using drugs or alcohol is not a solution but is only an additional problem.

4 Make a decision about getting help for your—or a friend's—eating disorder.

5 Stick to that decision and make a solid commitment for the future.

After you read this book, we hope that you will discover some answers to your questions about eating disorders and perhaps to some questions you hadn't even thought of yet. At the back of the book is a list of sources for further information, as well as a list of organizations you can contact for help. Thinking about the issues raised here is an important step toward making informed, responsible decisions about the way you eat and toward taking control of your own life.

Interview

Laura lives in a large city where she is now a freshman in college. She is recovering from an eating disorder that began in high school. She is in individual therapy and attends a group therapy session once a week. Therapy has allowed her to be more open and honest about her eating disorder. In this interview she describes how it began.

I remember the exact day I first became aware of how bad I felt about myself and my life. It was the day a poster was put up on the bulletin board at school about the spring dance. I knew I wanted to go, but I also knew I wouldn't. I hadn't been to a school dance in the three years I had been in high school.

That day when I got home, I went to my room and tried to do my homework. But I couldn't concentrate. I felt restless and dissatisfied. Nothing in my life was going right. I was feeling more irritable, and it was getting harder to hide it. I was angry, but I didn't know who I was angry at or why.

I left my homework on my desk and went over to the full-length mirror near my bed. I stood and looked at myself for a long time. Then I put on a little show—I smiled, I clowned, I posed like I was trying on different personalities. Suddenly for no reason I took off my clothes and stood there dressed only in my bra and panties. I was mortified by what I saw in the mirror. I only wore a size 9, but I looked more like a size 20. I hated the way I looked. All I saw in the mirror was disgusting layers of fat. No wonder I never went to the dances.

At dinner that night my younger sister Janet announced that she had been invited to the dance by Scott, who was in my class and was on the football team. My sister and my mother were laughing and happy about my sister's social conquest. (They have the same figure and thin waist. I look more like my dad, who is heavyset.) That's when I realized that my sister, who was two grades behind me, was passing me socially.

That day was a turning point. From then on I was determined to be thin, *very* thin. If being thin like my sister and mother was what it took to succeed, then that's what I was going to be. That night I vowed to myself to go on a strict diet and stick to it no matter what.

It worked. I began losing weight right away. One morning about a week later when I got off the scale I was ecstatic. I was naked and hadn't eaten anything in almost 24 hours. I hadn't even taken a sip of water. I wanted to be at my thinnest when I weighed myself. In just one week on my diet I went from 121 pounds to 107 pounds. Better yet, my weight loss was already beginning to show. My size 9 designer jeans were so loose I could actually slide them off without unbuttoning or unzipping them. My blue silk dress covered me like a tent.

In the weeks that followed, I spent a lot of time in front of the mirror watching this new person come into being. Although I was looking better—more like the people in the magazines—I still didn't like my body. I felt fat and ugly. In the past I always thought that if I could control my weight, I would be able to control my life and things would finally start going right for me.

One night when I opened the door, I smelled my mom's homemade garlic bread baking in the oven. I loved her garlic bread, and she knew it. After I started dieting, she made a point of cooking my favorite foods. Before, my mother used to try to get me not to overeat, but now she was doing everything she could to get me to eat. She took my diet as a personal challenge to her authority. Every night she made a point of serving some tasty dessert that would be difficult to refuse. Food became a battleground for my mother and me, and we both refused to surrender.

One night at dinner as I was picking at the tuna casserole, she threw down her napkin in disgust and let me have it. She yelled at me that I was making her sick. She went off on her kick that I didn't eat enough and I was turning into a scarecrow. She said I looked terrible and was getting worse every day.

I defended myself as best I could. I told her I didn't want to eat any more because I just wasn't hungry. My mother stood up and shook her finger at me. "You sit right there in your seat until you finish your meal. I don't want you to open your mouth again unless it's to put food into it." I had never seen her so mad. The veins in her neck were sticking out.

I knew better than to argue with my mother when she was like that. There was dead silence in the room. I took my fork and put some casserole in my mouth. I chewed it slowly while my parents watched. When I swallowed it, it tasted like sawdust. I drank lots of water to help me get the rest of the casserole down.

When the meal was finally over, I excused myself and went to my room. I took off my clothes and got into my terry-cloth bathrobe. I knew what I had to do, so I headed straight for the bathroom.

I turned on the faucets in the bathroom sink and turned on the water in the bathtub as well. Then I took off my robe and went to the toilet and lifted the seat. I knelt down and put my head over the bowl. Sticking my finger down my throat made me gag, but nothing happened. So I stuck my finger as far down as I could reach. Nausea came over me, and I vomited into the toilet. My throat felt sore and scratched, and my stomach muscles ached. Still, I forced myself to vomit several more times until I was sure I had thrown up all the food that I had eaten against my will.

That night as I was lying in bed before going to sleep, my mother came into my room. She sat on the edge of the bed and asked if I was still awake. She said she was sorry she got so angry at dinner. She told me she only wanted me to eat right and be healthy. She said she loved me, and I would always be her little girl.

As my mother sat there stroking my hair, I didn't know which one was my real mother—the one comforting me and saying she loved me or the one who was always getting mad at me. I wanted my mother's love more than anything in the world, but I just didn't know if she really loved me.

In the weeks and months that followed, my mother was happy I was eating more, although she still didn't like my skipping breakfast (she didn't know I skipped lunch at school, too). She was pleased that I ate the dinners she served, and as far as she was concerned, I was her good little dutiful daughter again.

Little did she know that after dinner upstairs in my bathroom I turned on the water faucets and vomited up what I ate. The longer I did it, the easier it got. Eventually I didn't even need my fingers. I just squeezed my stomach muscles and up came my mom's dinner.

But secrets can't be kept forever, and mine couldn't be either. Being found out was the best thing that ever happened to me. It allowed me to get into therapy and finally start dealing with my problems.

BULLETIN BOARD

An estimated 8 million people in the United States suffer from eating disorders.

The vast majority—more than 90%—of those afflicted with eating disorders are adolescent and young adult women.

About one-half of one percent (0.5%) of women between ages 10 and 30 have anorexia.

The overwhelming majority (95%) of anorexics are women.

As many as 1 in 250 young women have anorexia.

Approximately 1% of adolescent girls develop anorexia nervosa. 1 in 10 cases may lead to death from starvation, cardiac arrest, or suicide.

Another 2 to 3% of young women develop bulimia nervosa.

Half of people with anorexia also suffer from bulimia. Most of the 50% of bulimics who do not suffer from anorexia are of near-normal weight.

Though 40% of people with anorexia binge eat, many binge eaters do not develop anorexia.

Most women with anorexia and/or bulimia come from white, middle-class or upper-middle-class families.

About 5% of college-age women have bulimia.

14% of college-age women vomit at least occasionally to control their weight.

8% of college-age women use laxatives occasionally to control their weight.

Perhaps as many as 25% of the people in the United States overeat or exercise compulsively.

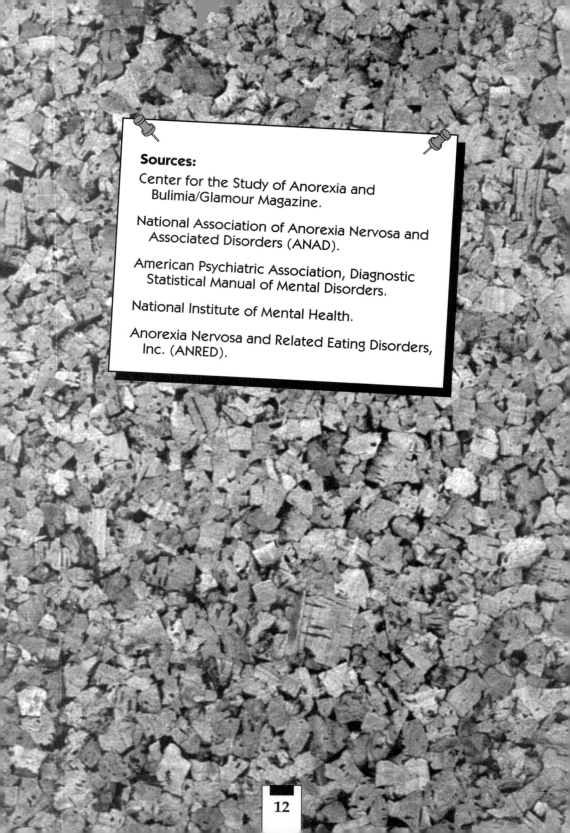

Sources:

Center for the Study of Anorexia and Bulimia/Glamour Magazine.

National Association of Anorexia Nervosa and Associated Disorders (ANAD).

American Psychiatric Association, Diagnostic Statistical Manual of Mental Disorders.

National Institute of Mental Health.

Anorexia Nervosa and Related Eating Disorders, Inc. (ANRED).

CHAPTER 1

Communicating

Q I can't talk to my mom because she gets too upset. I've been wanting to talk about my dieting, but she just criticizes me for not eating more. I just end up feeling worse. I wish my dad was around more, but he works all the time. He's nice. I wish I had somebody like him to talk to. But who wants to listen to me?

A Sounds like you're worried about the way you eat and need to talk to somebody about it. Most teens think about what they eat and care about how they look. It is natural to think about what you need to eat to look your best. However, if you worry about food, weight, and diet all the time, it may be a sign that you have or are developing a serious eating problem.

• • • • • • • • • • • •

Q Yes, I have to admit it. I do think about it a lot. I am really worried. But I don't know who to talk to. What should I do?

A Teenagers often find it difficult to talk to a parent about something like this, but there are lots of other people who can give you advice and information: teachers, counselors, relatives, friends—whomever you feel comfortable talking to. But if you can, you ought to try to talk to your parents, even though it might be hard. You'll open up lines of communication, and you and your parents will get a chance to understand one another's attitudes.

• • • • • • • • • • •

Q You just don't understand. My mom has this thing about food. She gets upset and emotional. I just can't talk to her.

A You may be surprised. She may very much want to talk to you. The idea that you have an eating problem probably worries her. She may have even discussed it with your dad. She may be looking for a chance to talk to you about it but just doesn't know how to bring it up without getting emotional. You might be doing yourself and

If you worry about your weight and diet all the time, you may have an eating disorder.

your family a big favor by bringing the subject up your-self. Since you seem to feel comfortable with your dad, you could ask for a family conference when he's around. But if that's too hard, if you're not yet ready to talk to your parents, choose somebody else to talk to.

• • • • • • • • • • • •

 I know I should talk to somebody, and I really want to. But I don't know, I guess I'm scared. I'm not sure why.

The sooner you can get the problem out into the open, the better. Most teens who suffer from eating disorders do it secretly. Breaking the silence is never easy. But it's the first step. You'll feel much better.

• • • • • • • • • • • •

Choosing Somebody to Talk To

The important thing is to find someone you trust. That person should be a good listener and should be nonjudgmental. You'll want the person to keep what you say confidential and to respect your feelings. Someone who makes what you're feeling seem unimportant isn't going to help you very much.

If you argue with one or both of your parents about the way you eat or if they disapprove of your eating habits, they may not be the best people to talk to, at least not in the beginning. It may be better to talk to somebody who is not so involved in the problem, like a teacher or friend. Also, you may want to talk to more than one person about your problem. It never hurts to get a "second opinion."

The very act of opening up to somebody else about your problem is part of the healing process. The more you can talk about your problem to others, the better off you will be.

Choosing a Good Time to Talk

Make sure you give yourself enough time. If you do talk to a parent, make sure enough time is set aside and your talk is not interrupted by phone calls or other family members. Make it clear that you need your parent's undivided attention.

If you plan on talking to a teacher or counselor, make an appointment. If you decide to talk to a friend or classmate you trust, don't do it in the lunchroom line or between classes. Having such an important conversation cut short will only disappoint you and make you feel frustrated.

Planning What You Want to Say

Collect your thoughts before the talk. Write down what you want to say, or make a list of the points you want to make.

Here are some suggestions:

■ Begin by telling the person that what you have to say is important and personal. If you want the person's promise that what you say is confidential, tell the person before you begin. Let the person know you thought he or she would be sympathetic and helpful.

■ Be honest. Tell the person that you are concerned that you have an eating problem, and you need help in dealing with it. Be specific. Do you skip meals? Are you terrified about getting fat? Whatever the problem is, don't minimize or make light of it. Don't hold back important information because you're embarrassed or ashamed. If you want, bring this book (or another book on eating disorders) with you to the talk, especially if you think it may help you make your points.

■ Be ready to talk about your feelings. Eating disorders are always about more than eating habits. The title of another book on eating disorders puts it well: *It's Not What You're Eating, It's What's Eating You.* When you have your conversation, be willing to talk about the things that are bothering you that may be driving you to eat the way you eat, whether that be overeating or undereating or eating in spurts or just worrying about what you eat all the time. Be prepared to talk about more than food.

■ Be prepared to follow through on the advice you receive. Don't be surprised if the person you talk to recommends therapy. If you have an eating disorder, you will need to get at the emotional problems that are behind it. Just getting a person to "eat right" does not solve the problem. Eating disorders are always evidence of other problems that need to be addressed. In fact, it is very difficult to recover from an eating disorder *without* some kind of therapy (see Chapter 7).

■ If your initial conversation with someone left you feeling that your concern was not taken seriously or that you were being judged or criticized, find another person to talk to. Once you talk to somebody about your problem, you are on your way to dealing with it. You should be proud of yourself. It takes courage to break the silence and bring the problem out in the open. This first conversation may be only a first step, but what a giant first step it will be.

CHAPTER 2

What Is an Eating Disorder?

Q Sometimes I feel so anxious that I think I'm going to jump out of my skin. That's when I most need to eat. I stuff myself even though I'm not hungry. I'll eat anything—potato chips, doughnuts, candy, cupcakes, ice cream. I know it's not good for me, but I do it anyway. It gives me something to do, and it makes me feel better. I just can't stop. I don't know why. Does that mean I have a problem?

A The problem is that you're eating for the wrong reason. You're eating not just to feed your body, but to deal with your anxiety. That's getting you into trouble. The fact that you say you can't stop is evidence that you are binge eating, which is one of the signs of an eating disorder. It is important that you look at the reasons you are binging. You need to think about why you get anxious. Underneath every eating disorder, there is an emotional problem that needs to be dealt with. Find somebody you can talk to about it.

* * * * * * * * * * *

Obsessive-Compulsive Behavior

If you have an eating disorder or are on your way to getting one, you are not alone. Many teenagers have serious eating problems. In fact, most eating disorders start during the teen years. They start when a teenager becomes so preoccupied with food, weight, and dieting that eating (or *not* eating) is the most important thing in the world—more important than friends, family, and schoolwork. Psychologically, such a preoccupation with eating belongs to a general group of disorders called obsessive-compulsive disorders. People with such disorders cannot control their behavior, and they often repeat certain actions, such as washing their hands or folding their clothes, without being able to stop themselves. These actions usually indicate emotional upset and are signs of inner struggles or repressed feelings.

Here are some of the harmful consequences of having an eating disorder:

■ *Health*: Eating disorders can lead to serious illness and sometimes even death.

■ *Relationships*: Teens with serious eating problems often become isolated from their classmates and family.

■ *Self-esteem*: Teens who develop eating disorders have underlying emotional problems.

Eating disorders are serious and dangerous. If you think you may have an eating problem or know somebody who does, you need to do something about it as soon as possible. The longer you wait, the more serious the disorder will become and the more difficult it will be to treat.

Food and Eating

Eating is essential, since food is what fuels our bodies. When our bodies don't get enough food, we experience the physical sensation of hunger. Hunger, which we usually experience as

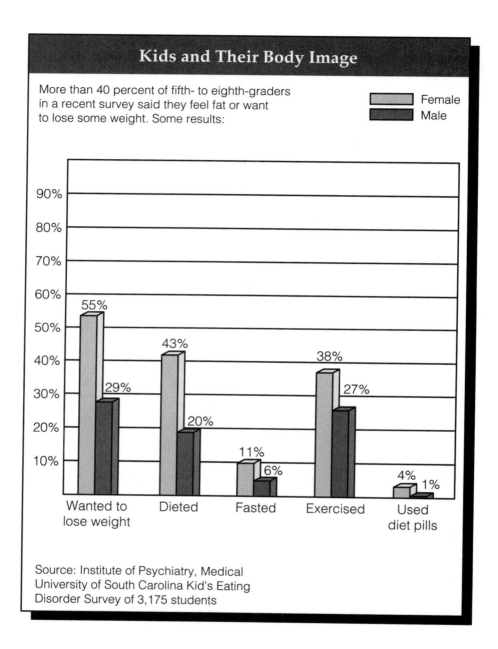

Kids and Their Body Image

More than 40 percent of fifth- to eighth-graders in a recent survey said they feel fat or want to lose some weight. Some results:

Female
Male

- Wanted to lose weight: 55%, 29%
- Dieted: 43%, 20%
- Fasted: 11%, 6%
- Exercised: 38%, 27%
- Used diet pills: 4%, 1%

Source: Institute of Psychiatry, Medical University of South Carolina Kid's Eating Disorder Survey of 3,175 students

gnawing feelings in the stomach, restlessness, and sometimes weakness, dizziness, or a headache, is a natural physical reaction to lack of food. It is the body's way of telling us it is low on fuel. When we eat something, the sensation of hunger passes and doesn't return until the body needs more fuel.

However, we don't just eat to satisfy hunger. We also eat to satisfy our appetite and desire for certain kinds of food because of their taste, smell, or look. Eating can satisfy both hunger and appetite at the same time.

The importance our society places on food and eating is one reason it is difficult for some people to deal with their eating problems. The preparation, presentation, and display of food have become an important part of our lives and our society. On radio and television, in newspapers and magazines, and at countless social functions, we are constantly encouraged to eat. Food is served at most family gatherings, social occasions, and holiday celebrations and is the main focus of many social gatherings—picnics, barbecues, dinner parties, and banquets. Food is also readily available at public events, such as movies, concerts, and sporting contests.

Many people are able to deal successfully with this abundance of food and food advertising in their lives. For such people, food and eating are a natural part of their lives, like walking or sleeping. However, for many others, food becomes the most important thing in their lives. When people think so much about food, they will tend to overeat; overeating almost inevitably leads to dieting—one of *the* great American pastimes today—and, sometimes, to an obsession with overweight.

Thin Is In

Preoccupation both with food and dieting is so much a part of our culture that it is not unusual to find teenagers, especially girls, who are seriously concerned about adding even a pound or two above their desired weight. The message they get is clear: thin is in! The magazines they read bombard them with pictures of slim, long-legged models, glamorous movie stars, and articles on exercise and staying thin (of course, the same magazines also feature recipes for gourmet foods and rich desserts and tips for serving dishes attractively). Young men are also invited to be conscious of their waistlines through ads showing handsome and slender joggers, body builders, fitness enthusiasts, and users of cosmetics for men.

No matter that most of us do not fit the body type of these images! Of course, no amount of dieting could ever produce such incredibly desirable models out of ordinary people! Fashion is all. It may have reflected a different taste in the past, to which the softer, voluptuous figures of a Marilyn Monroe or a Jane Russell attest. But today, to the apparent great anxiety of a lot of us, many who are successful in gaining money and romance are above all *thin*.

Looking in the Mirror

When you look in the mirror, what do you see? Are you satisfied with what you see? Do you have positive feelings about your body shape, size, and the way you look? Or do you find it hard to accept yourself as you are and find yourself feeling anxious or self-critical?

Many teens who look in the mirror don't like what they see because they think they weigh too much. They cannot accept their natural body shape or the changes that are happening to them as they grow. They may think that because they don't look like thin people, they are unacceptable. Teens have trouble knowing who they are, so they try to manufacture themselves to be what the media says they should be. They may also be anxious that they don't fit the image their peers prefer.

If being thin is important to your friends, you'll probably accept that value as your own. The problem is that many if not most people aren't built to be thin. For them, trying to be thin like the models in the advertisements can be a real problem. You may even end up feeling mistakenly foolish or inadequate if you misjudge how others see you.

What Causes Eating Disorders?

Most experts agree that there is no single or main cause of serious eating problems. Instead, many factors go into the creation of an eating disorder. Children come from families where any of a number of serious problems can occur—for example, serious financial difficulties, alcoholism, depression, sexual abuse, or lack of emotional care. Still, while people with eating disorders vary when it comes to personality, age, gender, and family background, they do tend to have many things in common.

In the past, people admired the soft, full figure of a star like Marilyn Monroe. Today, fashion dictates that people strive for a thin, streamlined body.

Almost always, eating problems begin with failed attempts to control or deal with weight gain, and such problems grow in response to feelings of depression and inadequacy. Teens with eating problems are usually convinced they're ugly, worthless, and untalented. Often they believe that everything bad or disappointing in life is a punishment for their inadequacy.

Eating-disorder experts believe that our society's emphasis on thinness is harmful to young people. Fear of being fat and the desire to be thin drive many teens to lose weight even if they are only slightly overweight or not overweight at all.

The pressure on girls to be thin is especially strong. "From adolescence onward females are more greatly affected than males by the climate of prejudice against fatness," said one psychologist. "In this climate large numbers of women are more likely to develop eating disorders."

Danger Signals

Since the physical changes you are going through now are indeed major ones, growing into your adult body can be an exciting experience. But it also can be a frustrating one because you can never be sure how it's all going to turn out, or how you're going to end up looking. If you accept how you look right now without feeling disappointed in yourself, you probably are not in danger of developing an eating disorder. However, if you are unhappy with the difference between the way you want to look and the way you actually look, and if you feel bad about yourself generally, you are a prime candidate for an eating disorder. You may soon be headed for possible trouble if:

Many teenage girls are unhappy unless they look just like the models they see in magazines.

■ You accept the "thin is in" attitude and try to achieve that image at all costs.

■ Your body image is a major and constant source of disappointment to you.

■ You don't give yourself credit for the things you're good at.

■ You believe that you're never good enough or smart enough.

■ You keep your emotions hidden.

■ You often think "Who could like me?"

You don't have to like or love yourself all the time. But if you rarely or never do and have trouble believing anybody else could feel positively about you, you are in danger of setting yourself up for a possible eating disorder.

Fear of Fatness

Fear of having a fat body is something all people with eating disorders have in common. They may be overweight because they eat too many fattening foods or eat too much in general, or they may be terrified of becoming obese (having an excessive amount of fatty tissue). People are considered obese if they are 25 percent or more above their ideal weight, which is the weight doctors consider to be healthiest for an individual, taking into account height, body frame, and age.

The fear of being fat is what drives many teens and others to begin dieting. Experts estimate that in the United States alone more than 80 million people are on some kind of diet, and they spend $300 million a year on diet products.

People who diet may succeed in losing the desired amount of weight at first, but they almost always gain it back and then some. Studies show that less than 2 percent of overweight people who go on diets reach their goal and keep the weight off. The vast majority lose a few pounds, then go off the diet and gain the weight back again.

Eating disorders may develop when people become habitual dieters, constantly gaining and then losing weight. Often their desperate need to change their body image drives them to diets and other methods of weight loss. As these attempts to lose weight fail, they resort to more and more extreme methods of weight control.

Constant dieting is unhealthy not only because it creates an irregular eating pattern, but also because it actually increases the desire for food. The more dieters deprive themselves of food, the more they crave it and the more obsessed they

Facts About Dieting

☐ After two years, 95% of dieters regain all their lost weight plus about 10 extra pounds.

☐ After five years, 98% of dieters regain all their lost weight plus about 10 extra pounds.

☐ Americans spend over $300 million a year on diet products.

☐ 80% of the female population has dieted before reaching age 18.

☐ 90% of junior and senior high school girls diet.

☐ Only about 10% of high school girls are overweight.

☐ 49% of college-age women follow diets of 800 calories a day or less. Semi-starvation is 1,200 calories a day. The average normal-weight woman eats 1,800–2,200 calories a day. The average normal-weight man eats 2,600–3,000 calories a day.

☐ Women need a fat level of approximately 22% of their body weight in order to menstruate normally.

☐ 100% of dieters are tempted to binge eat because they are hungry.

Sources: Anorexia Nervosa and Related Eating Disorders (ANRED); Center for the Study of Anorexia and Bulimia/Glamour Magazine.

become with the idea of eating. Eventually they give in to their urges and eat whatever they crave. Because they have been so deprived, they may binge, eating large amounts of food at one time. This pattern of binging and dieting is a central feature of most eating disorders.

Do You Have an Eating Disorder?

Since eating and dieting are such a part of the way we live, it is sometimes not so easy to tell which teens have eating disorders and which don't. After all, don't most teens care about their weight and how they look?

If you worry about food and weight so much that it is the main thing you think about and it affects the way you eat, then you most likely have a problem. You certainly do if the way you feel about yourself—and school, friends, and family—depends on what you have or have not eaten and how much you weigh.

Eating disorders involve excessive worry about weight, binge-eating, frequent dieting, compulsive exercising, fasting, and other behaviors that focus on eating, purging (cleaning out), or avoiding food. As a result, relationships with friends, family, and other people suffer, and communication ceases being two-way, sometimes stopping altogether.

Do you suspect you may have an eating disorder? Take this quiz and find out. Answer the following questions as accurately as you can. Be honest—you're doing it for yourself.

■ Do you eat when you're not hungry?

■ Do you feel guilty or sad after you eat?

■ Do you eat to block out worries or troubles?

■ Do you think about food too much?

■ Does the way you eat make you or your parents unhappy?

■ Do you feel fat even though people tell you you're thin?

■ Do you get anxious and depressed if you gain weight?

■ Do you get nervous when people watch you eat?

■ Do you have a secret stash of food?

■ Do you eat normally in front of others and then binge when you're alone?

■ Do you eat lots of junk food?

■ Do you pass up dances or other social events because you don't like the way you look?

If you answered yes to one or more of these questions, you need to keep reading. If you decide you have an eating disorder or are on your way to developing one, be assured that eating disorders can be treated and overcome. The fact that you are reading this book is a good start.

In the next three chapters, you will learn about the three major eating disorders—anorexia, bulimia, and compulsive overeating. Bulimics and compulsive overeaters eat large amounts of food in short periods of time, while anorexics eat so little they become dangerously thin. While the eating disorders you will read about are closely related as part of the same general pattern of harmful, disordered eating, each one has its own distinct symptoms and behaviors.

CHAPTER 3

Anorexia

Q I like being thin. If I wasn't as thin as I am, probably nobody would pay attention to me. I would be just another nobody. Besides, I like watching what I eat and looking as thin as the models in the magazines. I diet all the time. What's wrong with that?

A It sounds as if you may be starving yourself to achieve a certain look. To get people's attention, you are trying to force your body to look thin when that may not be what it wants. You are hurting yourself when you deprive your body of the food it needs. You should allow yourself to look like you—the *natural* you—not like some model in a magazine. You could be headed toward the most dangerous of all the eating disorders.

• • • • • • • • • • • •

The Dieter's Disease

Teenagers who starve themselves on purpose suffer from an eating disorder called *anorexia nervosa*. Anorexia is sometimes called "the starvation sickness" or "the dieter's disease." The disorder often begins in adolescence and involves severe weight loss—15 percent or more of the person's normal body weight. Many young women with the disorder look emaciated, even though they are convinced they are overweight. While the disorder mostly affects teenage girls (over 90 percent of anorexics are female), boys and young men also suffer from anorexia—and their number is growing. If not treated in its early stages, anorexia will become a severe, chronic illness that requires hospitalization. In the most extreme cases, it can also cause death.

Thinness at Any Cost

Nancy developed anorexia when she was 15. She was worried that she wasn't pretty enough to get boys' attention, especially since she was slightly overweight. When her father jokingly told her she would never get a date unless she slimmed down, she went on a strict diet. She kept at it, never believing she was thin enough, even after she became extremely underweight.

Nancy thought about dieting and food all the time. She stopped menstruating and developed strange eating rituals. Every morning she weighed the food she was going to eat that day on a kitchen scale. Then she cut the food up into tiny pieces and precisely measured the liquids she planned to drink. She put her small food ration for the day in small containers and lined them up in neat rows. She also exercised vigorously several times a day, even when she felt faint.

Finally, the family doctor insisted that she enter the hospital and be closely monitored. But even in the hospital, Nancy kept up her exercising in secret by locking herself in the bathroom and doing strenuous sets of sit-ups. Only after several more hospitalizations and a great deal of individual and family therapy was Nancy able to recover.

Afraid to Gain Weight

Nancy's case is not unusual. Teens with anorexia think nothing of starving themselves, even though they experience severe hunger pains. What is worrisome about the disorder is that anorexics are convinced they're overweight, even after they have lost so much weight that they are skin and bones.

However, extreme dieting is an acute assault on the human

body. The self-starvation that characterizes anorexia causes severe and permanent physical damage and can be fatal. *Up to 10 percent of anorexics die.*

Symptoms of Anorexia

Anorexics often refuse to eat in front of other people. Like Nancy, they may exercise compulsively to keep themselves from gaining weight. Loss of monthly menstrual periods is very common in females with the disorder. Anorexic males often become impotent.

Frequently an anorexic will start with a normal diet but then eliminate foods from it day by day. If she can do this, she feels happy that she is making progress toward her goals. If she can't cut back, she will feel bad and hate herself "for being such a pig." Even though the anorexic refuses to eat, her need for food makes her think about it all the time. Many anorexics will even hide and hoard the food that they refuse to eat.

How do you know if you have anorexia? If you think you or somebody you know might suffer from it, here are some symptoms to look for:

■ Loss of a significant amount of weight

■ Dieting although thin

■ Feeling fat even after losing weight

■ Constant denial of being hungry; claiming to be "full" after only a few bites

■ Odd eating habits, such as weighing and measuring food, cutting food into tiny pieces

■ Feeling cold

A person with anorexia is convinced she is overweight, even when her weight is normal. When she looks in the mirror, all she sees is fat.

■ Dressing in layers to hide weight loss

■ Strong and frequent feelings of insecurity, loneliness, inadequacy, and helplessness

■ Denial that anything is wrong; becoming sullen, defensive, or angry when others express concern

What People with Anorexia Think

People with anorexia think about food, weight, and thinness most of the time and often share common thought patterns. If you are anorexic, here are some thoughts you might be having:

■ "I'm a worthless nobody. I don't have anything special about me. Nobody pays attention to me."

■ "I can never live up to my parents' expectations of me. I'm always at fault."

■ "I'm too fat. I'll be much happier if I lose weight."

■ "Being thin is the most important thing in the world."

■ "Gaining weight is terrible. And if I let it happen, I'm a terrible person."

■ "I'm not hungry. Nothing is wrong. I'm in control."

How Anorexia Begins

How does such a dangerous eating disorder begin? Certainly a girl who is painfully thin and who may be close to death did not set out to become anorexic. Like many teens, she simply wanted to go on a diet to lose weight. But as she diets and sheds pounds, she begins to feel a new sense of strength and control. As she loses more weight, looks better to herself, and does not give in to her hunger, she suddenly feels more powerful. She discovers she doesn't have to eat as other people do.

Jenny's Story

As Jenny, age 16, discovered the feeling of power that came from losing weight, her dieting became more and more extreme. Five feet four inches tall, she gained 25 pounds in the six months after she broke up with her boyfriend. After the breakup she withdrew from friends, stayed home, and overate until she reached 145 pounds. That's when she panicked at her weight gain and stopped eating.

At home she picked at her food, calculating how many calories were in each bite. She ate only salads and then figured out how many hours of exercise she needed to do to work off the calories. Sometimes she'd stay up and exercise for hours before she was satisfied she had burned off enough calories. In just six weeks she lost all the weight she had gained, as well as 15 additional pounds. Even though she weighed only 105 pounds, she still wanted to lose more weight.

Although Jenny had not yet lost 15 to 20 percent of her normal body weight, she was definitely showing signs of anorexia—refusal to eat, imagining herself overweight despite being underweight, and her preoccupation with food and exercise. Jenny continued losing weight for another six months, until finally individual therapy and family therapy helped her reverse her weight loss.

Gaining Control

Dieting and weight control are what give meaning to the anorexic's life. Every day becomes a challenge. The number on the scale becomes the most important number in her life, more important than grades or sports scores. The excitement of this challenge and the new sense of self-control are hard to give up.

The reason many teens become anorexic is that they have not

found other ways to feel in control of their lives. Often the anorexic is the typical "good girl" who grew up being a model child. To win the approval of others, she learned to put the needs of others ahead of her own.

Now, perhaps for the first time in her life, she feels a sense of importance as she loses weight and carefully monitors her food intake. She has found a way to tell her family and the world that she's going to eat what *she* wants to eat, not what others tell her to eat. For the normally shy "good girl," this new sense of power is exciting and not easy to give up, especially if her parents and others are trying to pressure her to give it up.

Dangerous Denial
One of the most common and disturbing features of anorexia is the stubborn denial that anything is wrong. The anorexic denies she is hungry and ignores the physical problems that accompany the disorder—dehydration, dizziness, low blood pressure, numbness of the hands and feet, and heart problems. Anorexics will fiercely resist the idea of therapy because they view all attempts to help them as ways to get them to eat.

As a result of the ferocity of the anorexic's denial that anything's wrong and her zealous commitment to the disorder, the progression of anorexia can be tragic. An alarming number of anorexics die. Anorexia is an acute disorder that can last anywhere from a few months to many years.

Physical Effects of Prolonged Dieting

The physical consequences of self-starvation are serious. The longer anorexia is allowed to continue, the more dangerous it becomes. Here are some of the physical consequences:

■ Stopping of menstrual cycle

■ Lower body temperature

In addition to extreme dieting, the anorexic person may pursue a rigorous and compulsive program of exercise.

■ Low blood pressure and slower pulse

■ Smaller, weaker heart

■ Low estrogen, leading to osteoporosis

■ Loss of muscle mass

■ Paleness

■ Bluish hands and feet (acrocyanosis)

■ Growth of fine body hair (lanugo)

■ Poor nail quality and hair texture (dull, brittle, thin)

■ Dizziness and fainting spells

■ Insomnia

■ Constipation

■ Slowed metabolism and slower reflexes

Dieting Safely

If you want to lose weight, you should not change the way you eat on your own. You should talk to somebody—your parents, school nurse, or guidance counselor—and ask them to schedule an appointment for you to see a doctor or registered dietician (that is, an expert in nutrition) to plan a safe and effective diet.

While you are in your teens, your growing body has special nutritional needs that most fad diets will not meet. Dieting can produce an eating disorder because it leads to rebound weight gain. That occurs when the dieter loses weight for a while only to gain back even more weight as soon as she or he goes off the diet. Diets that are too restrictive and don't meet your nutritional needs can lead to serious health problems and interfere with your body's normal development.

If you want to lose weight, here are some things you should remember:

■ Ask your school nurse to help you find a doctor or dietician who can help you plan a safe, effective diet.

■ With the doctor or dietician, target a sensible weight range and plan a sensible diet that will help you reach your goal.

■ Eat nutritious, balanced meals.

■ Avoid junk food.

■ Maintain a healthy program of regular exercise or physical activity.

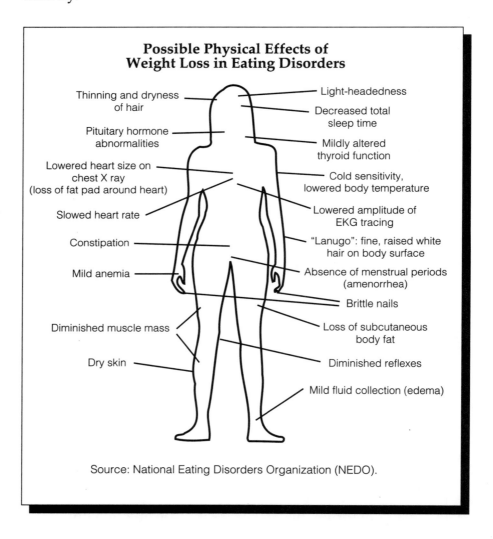

**Possible Physical Effects of
Weight Loss in Eating Disorders**

Thinning and dryness of hair

Pituitary hormone abnormalities

Lowered heart size on chest X ray
(loss of fat pad around heart)

Slowed heart rate

Constipation

Mild anemia

Diminished muscle mass

Dry skin

Light-headedness

Decreased total sleep time

Mildly altered thyroid function

Cold sensitivity, lowered body temperature

Lowered amplitude of EKG tracing

"Lanugo": fine, raised white hair on body surface

Absence of menstrual periods (amenorrhea)

Brittle nails

Loss of subcutaneous body fat

Diminished reflexes

Mild fluid collection (edema)

Source: National Eating Disorders Organization (NEDO).

CHAPTER 4

Bulimia

Q I diet hard to get my weight down, but then I ruin everything by going on a binge. I feel terrible that all my dieting is for nothing. But at least I have a way of not putting on weight. I just throw up what I eat, so it doesn't turn into fat. I know it's sort of disgusting. But it works. Does that mean something's wrong with me?

A Well, you're finding out that strict dieting doesn't work. Recent studies show that most people end up gaining back the weight they lose, and sometimes more. It must also occur to you that you're going through an awful lot of unpleasantness to keep your weight down. You've become caught up in the self-defeating binge/purge cycle that is known as *bulimia nervosa*. Yes, I'd say you have an eating disorder.

• • • • • • • • • • • •

The Binge/Purge Cycle

People with bulimia go through cycles of starving themselves, then eating a large amount of food in a short period of time, and then "purging" themselves (or cleaning themselves out) by vomiting or taking laxatives. Most bulimics binge and purge in secret. They maintain their normal or slightly above normal body weight and may hide their problem from others for long periods of time.

As is the case with anorexics, the vast majority of bulimics are female. However, unlike anorexia, which usually begins in the early teens, bulimia usually begins in the mid- or late teens. Many bulimics begin as anorexics but break out of that pattern when they start to binge and purge. It is believed that half of those with anorexia will eventually develop bulimia.

The Binge

The size of the binge varies depending on the food and the finances available. Some teens will binge only occasionally, while others may binge for a major part of the day. When money is not available, a bulimic may even steal food. Binging may be planned ahead of time, or it may be unplanned. Once a binge begins, a bulimic will do almost anything for food—raid the kitchen, go to a grocery store, or order food from a pizzeria or restaurant.

Karen, age 16, told how when she went on vacations with her parents, she'd steal food from the room service carts in the hallway of the hotel where they stayed. Melissa, age 17, said, "Once I start binging, it's like being drunk. Nothing else matters."

Shame and Guilt

The binge leaves the person feeling exhausted and full of shame and guilt. She can't believe she's acted that way and despises herself for being such a needy, out-of-control person. Bulimics tend to be perfectionists and are very hard on themselves. They live in fear of gaining weight from a binge. They fear that any extra pounds will expose them as somebody who binges and loses control.

The Purge

The purge can take many forms, but most often it involves self-induced vomiting or taking laxatives. Other forms of purging include using diuretics (medicines to increase the output of urine), emetics (medicines to induce vomiting), enemas, and diet pills. Compulsive exercising (that is, exercising that is lengthy, demanding, sometimes excessive, and uncontrollable) often accompanies the purge. The amount of purging varies from person to person. Some people binge and vomit a few times a month, while others do it several times a day. Some may even vomit in the middle of a binge so they can continue eating. Most vomit only after all the food has been eaten.

For most bulimics, purging is their solution for their loss of control over food. As Helen, age 18, puts it: "When I binge, I lose. When I purge, the food loses." Most bulimics vomit by using their fingers or a spoon handle. However, after repeated vomiting the esophageal muscles (in the tube connecting the mouth with the stomach) relax so much that many bulimics don't have to do anything more than tighten their stomachs to bring up the food.

Bulimics who have trouble vomiting may use laxatives, but they are ineffective. Laxatives give only an illusion of weight loss since they work after the food has already been digested and the calories absorbed. Still, many laxative abusers continue the practice as a way of feeling thinner.

Bulimia and Men

Although bulimia occurs mostly in young women, it is also found in young men. Some male athletes—wrestlers, for example—resort to purging, or more often, extreme exercising, to reach a weight limit for their sport, and then they binge. However, a wrestler usually does not have a distorted image of his body and returns to his normal weight when not competing. High school coaches, however, are becoming watchful for bulimics among their athletes so that they can head off unhealthy behavior.

Shameful Secret

Patty developed bulimia at the age of 17. As with most eating disorders, her problem began with dieting. She dieted severely

Occasional, social food binges may be normal for some girls. For others, binging becomes a secret ritual that follows strict dieting and can lead to bulimia. A bulimic in this group would be ashamed if the others knew about it.

to try to keep her weight down. Whenever she went off her diet and ate a large amount of food, she would force herself to vomit up the food.

When things did not go well for Patty, she experienced a powerful craving for sweets. Having learned how to purge her food, she would give in to her craving by eating large amounts of candy and cake until she felt stuffed and utterly exhausted and her stomach ached. Overwhelmed with guilt and disgust, she would then go to the bathroom and vomit up all the sweets she had just eaten.

Unable to understand her behavior, Patty became frightened, angry, and depressed. She felt isolated and lonely, convinced that nobody else would understand or approve of her behavior. Since her weight stayed within her normal range, nobody else knew anything was wrong.

Finally, she became so depressed that she tried to commit

suicide. While recuperating in the hospital, she was referred to an eating-disorders clinic. There Patty received medication for her illness and entered group therapy where she received the understanding and help she needed from others who have the same problem.

Although bulimia typically begins in the late teen years, it often continues for many years afterward because it is so hard to detect. People with the disorder often do not seek help until they reach their thirties or forties. By then, their eating habits are deeply ingrained and very difficult to change. In clinical terms, when disturbed eating behavior exists for several years, it becomes either chronic or intermittent.

How Bulimia Develops

Bulimia often begins when a teenager is under tension, usually associated with a change or a disappointment, such as a new school or the breakup of a relationship. The teen turns to food for comfort and escape from stress or upset and eventually gains weight. Dieting is followed by binging and purging. The behavior outwardly appears to be a way for a teen to be in con-trol—of her eating, her weight, her shape, her image—but unfortunately it most often ends up in an out-of-control cycle of binging and purging.

Food As an Emotional Outlet

Teens with bulimia use food as an emotional outlet. They have little confidence in themselves and tend to hide their anger and other negative feelings from themselves and others. They depend on others for approval and judge their worthiness by the standards of others. Eating becomes a way for them to deal with all the turmoil and upset that's inside them.

As bulimia develops, the teen thinks more and more about eating and purging. She begins to organize her life around eat-ing—when she'll eat, what she'll eat, how she's going to get rid of the calories. What started out as an attempt to control her body and weight has become a disorder that rules her life.

Trying Not to Binge

Some bulimics go to great lengths not to binge. They may put Ajax or Tide on the food they don't want to eat, dump the food in the garbage, or have somebody lock it up or hide it. But this seldom works. Bulimics end up washing the food, getting it out of the garbage, or finding it no matter where it's hidden. The teen's struggle not to binge becomes as intense as the struggle of any drug addict trying to kick the drug habit.

Every day during her first months in college, Barbara, age 17, made a vow to be "good" that day. "Not today," she would tell herself. "Today I won't binge."

Barbara usually made it through the day to dinner without breaking her vow, but she always had a tough time getting through the evening. When she went to bed with her vow still

Purging, or vomiting what has just been eaten, follows the binge. Unless the disorder is treated early, the bulimic may struggle with the disorder indefinitely.

intact, she would lie in bed for hours, unable to sleep. Inevitably she would get up and eat her roommate's food or go downstairs to the dorm candy machines. Even if she only ate one muffin or one candy bar, she would vomit it up so it wouldn't be in her stomach and keep her awake.

"What kills me is that every day for three years I was doing this," she said, "starting out 'good' and then blowing it every night. Do you know how that made me feel? I felt like something crazy was happening to me."

Bulimics are very hard on themselves. Instead of seeing themselves as having a disorder that can and needs to be treated, they think of themselves as failures and hate themselves for their weakness. Unlike the anorexic, they may turn to drugs or alcohol to escape from their unhappiness, thus compounding their problems.

Unless bulimia is treated early during the teen years, it will become an illness in which more and more of a person's life revolves around the struggle with food. However, unlike the anorexic, the bulimic knows she's hurting herself. Because she knows something is wrong, she is more likely than the anorexic to seek help. Furthermore, complications that lead to death are less common in bulimia.

When bulimia is accompanied by anorexia, however, the outcome may be tragic, as was the case with gymnast Christy Henrich, who died at age 22 in July 1994. The cause of her death was multiple organ system failure. Henrich had long suffered from both anorexia and bulimia and weighed only 61 pounds when she died. Failing to make the U.S. Olympic team in 1988 by only a fraction of a point, Henrich was a very hard-driving competitor affected by a health problem facing many women athletes today. Not only gymnasts are affected, but also swimmers, distance runners, tennis and volleyball players, divers, and figure skaters. In these sports, great importance is attached to weight and often to appearance. The American College of Sports Medicine reports that as many as 62 percent of females in such sports have eating disorders.

What to Look For

If you think you or somebody you know might be suffering from bulimia, here are the things to look for:

■ Strict dieting and constant preoccupation with body weight and shape

■ Binging, or eating uncontrollably, often in secret

■ Purging by vomiting; by abusing laxatives, diuretics, emetics, or diet pills; or by exercising vigorously

■ Preference for high-fat, high-sugar binge foods

■ Frequent use of bathroom after meals

■ Sudden disappearance of large amounts of food

■ Depression or mood swings

■ Fear of discovery

■ Problem with alcohol or drugs

Here are some of the thoughts shared by many bulimics:

■ "When I start to eat, it feels like I'm not going to stop."

■ "I want to stop binging and purging, but I'm afraid I'll gain weight if I do."

■ "Being attractive is very important to me."

Physical Consequences of Binging and Purging

Binging and purging are definitely bad for your health. Here are some of the consequences:

■ Heartburn, bloating, abdominal pain and cramps, internal bleeding, vomiting blood, indigestion, gas, constipation

■ Electrolyte imbalance that can lead to weakness, rapid or irregular heartbeat, cardiac arrest

■ Swollen cheek glands

■ Irregular menstrual periods

■ Liver and kidney damage

■ Frequent weight fluctuations

■ Sore throats

■ Dental and/or throat problems caused by stomach acids in vomiting

■ Broken blood vessels in face and under eyes

■ Dehydration, fainting spells, tremors, blurred vision

■ Fatigue and aching muscles

■ Damage to bowels

Losing Weight Safely

If you and your doctor decide you should diet, he or she will help you do it safely and in a way that helps you take the weight off and keep it off.

Warnings About Medications

Never use any weight-loss medication, including diet pills, to reduce your appetite unless your doctor specifically tells you to do so. Any diet pills that reduce your appetite should only be used under a doctor's supervision and only for a short time.

Read the label on all medications you take and follow the directions exactly as written. Use the medicine only for the reason stated on the label. If there is something on a medicine label you don't understand, ask somebody. Not following directions can be dangerous.

Never use laxatives, diuretics, or emetics as a way to lose weight, even temporarily. If you read the label, you'll know you should never do that.

Side Effects

If you have any side effects after taking any medicine, stop taking the medicine immediately and talk with your parents, a doctor, or your school nurse. And never take more medication than the label instructs.

Interview

Jimmy is now in high school. He has had an eating problem and has been overweight most of his life. He has tried losing weight many times, but it never really worked. Whenever he lost a few pounds, he always gained it back and then some. In junior high school he began attending Overeaters Anonymous meetings, and he now is in his second year of individual therapy. In this interview, he tells his story.

When I was born, there was something wrong with my stomach. I couldn't eat the way I was supposed to. This worried my parents because I wasn't gaining weight the way I was supposed to. The doctor said my stomach wasn't developed yet.

For a long time my parents had to feed me special food with a teaspoon. They did this until I finally could eat on my own. Naturally, my ability to eat pleased my mom and dad very much. They were so happy, they kept encouraging me to eat, even after my stomach problem was over. I ate and ate and became very fat.

When I was about seven, two of my cousins came to visit us for the summer. Whenever I tried to play or do something with them and my sister, they said things like "You're too fat to do this." They called me Tubby, and the name stuck. Once when we were playing baseball, I swung at the ball so hard I almost fell down. My cousin, Jake, yelled, "Hey, Tubby, don't fall down or you'll cause a big earthquake." They all laughed at me. I tried to pretend I didn't hear the things they said, but it hurt bad when my own family insulted me.

In elementary school I wasn't as fat as I got later because I was still growing, but I still was pretty miserable. I don't know if I was miserable because I was fat or fat because I was miserable. I guess I felt sorry for myself. It didn't seem fair that I was the only fat one in my family. My brother, who is five grades ahead of me, was always somebody everybody talked about. Every year my new teachers begin by telling me what a great student and great athlete he is. He played high school baseball, football, basketball, you name it. He had the kind of body I was supposed to have.

The older I got, the worse things got. Even my mom and dad started criticizing me and getting on my case about my weight. My sister always said bad things. Whenever she got mad, she called me "Blimpo" or "Fatbutt" or something like that. She liked making up new names to call me. Even my teacher talked to me about my "overeating problem."

My mom tried to give me smaller portions at dinner, but that didn't make much difference, since I ate mostly between meals. Sometimes I ate so much in the afternoon I wasn't all that hungry at dinnertime. For lunch in the school cafeteria, I usually went back for seconds and thirds. It got to be a school joke—how much I could put away. Actually, I liked the attention. I used to show off about how much I could eat. The more kidding I took, the more I ate. I guess I liked getting attention better than being ignored.

After school, kids would follow me to McDonald's just to see me eat more. I usually stopped off and had a couple of cheeseburgers, a double order of fries, and a chocolate milk shake. At dinner I didn't have to eat as much, which pleased my parents. For a while there they thought I was on a diet.

When I look back on it now, I'm embarrassed at the way I played the role of the fat clown. I guess by making my eating a joke and turning myself into a clown, it was my way of protecting myself.

It seems I was always trying to diet. My last year in elementary school, I was determined to lose a whole bunch of pounds so I could go to junior high school and be thinner and not have to go through it all again for another three years. I didn't want to put up with what I had gone through with four times as many kids.

I stopped going to McDonald's after school for a long time, and I didn't let the other kids dare me into show-off eating. But the trouble was that without my usual afternoon "snack" after school I was so hungry when I got home, I raided the fridge before my mother got home from her job. I made sandwiches and gobbled up everything sweet in sight.

My plan to slim down before going to junior high school was a flop. By seventh grade, I was the fattest I had ever been. The whole thing started up again my very first day. A ninth grader who was with a big group of his classmates coming down the hall pointed at me and shouted, "How ya doing rolypoly?" They all laughed, and that became one of my new nicknames. That afternoon, I went to McDonald's and had three cheeseburgers. I don't know who I was really trying to hurt. I certainly wasn't hurting those ninth graders. I was only hurting myself.

The day I walked through the door into my first OA meeting was the most important day of my life. I was scared, and everybody in the room looked weird. At first I felt like running out of there as fast as I could. But I stayed, and I'm glad I did. All these people who looked so weird were very honest when they spoke. Each person who said something began by admitting he or she had a disease and needed help. I didn't say anything. I just listened.

After a while, the leader asked who was at the meeting for the first time. I raised my hand along with a woman on the other side of the room. When everybody clapped and smiled and said things that made me feel welcome, I was glad I came. By the end of the first meeting, the people didn't look as weird anymore. Many of them came up to me after the meeting and encouraged me to come back. I said I would, and I did.

At the next meeting I got up my nerve to raise my hand. When I was called on, I began, "Hi, I'm Jimmy and I eat too much." I don't remember what I said, but I said pretty much what I told you, beginning with my birth and why my parents encouraged me to eat. At the end of the meeting, people came up and thanked me for sharing my story. That day two eighth-grade girls were there. One was as fat as I was, and the other one, her friend, was overweight, but not as much.

I've been going to meetings pretty much ever since. As I felt more comfortable at the meetings, I talked more about the things that really bothered me. When I began to realize that my problems were not just about eating but about the way I thought about myself, my parents encouraged me to talk to a therapist, and I do.

With the help of both my therapist and OA, I'm definitely changing. I don't feel as isolated as I used to feel, and now I have friends for the first time in my life. I have school friends, and I have my OA friends.

I'm still working on my weight problem, but I've made a lot of progress. I like talking to my therapist. I also like my OA meetings. OA people don't just talk about how much they eat or weigh. They talk about things that bother them and how they feel. I like being able to say what's on my mind.

CHAPTER 5

Compulsive Overeating

Q I wouldn't mind having a girlfriend, but I feel shy and unsure of myself whenever I'm around girls. I'm afraid they'll make fun of me for being fat. That's what I like about food. It doesn't mock me or laugh at me or make me feel bad. Food helps me feel better. Is there anything wrong with that?

A If you are self-conscious about your weight and unsure of yourself when it comes to girls, you should find somebody to talk to about it. Talking to somebody about what's bothering you will help you much more than eating too much.

• • • • • • • • • • •

Compulsive overeating is a pattern of episodes of uncontrolled eating, followed by feelings of guilt and shame about eating so much or eating the "wrong" kind of food (ice cream, cake, candy, chocolate, junk food). This often leads to dieting or fasting to make up for the overeating. But this food deprivation inevitably leads to another round of overeating. Because compulsive overeaters usually eat in binges, their disorder is also often called binge eating disorder.

Overeating Compulsively

Do you feel out of control when you eat? Do you sometimes eat without knowing why you are eating? Do you eat large amounts of food and don't stop until you feel stuffed?

Teens who overeat have a much harder time losing weight and keeping it off than teens with bulimia. Since overeaters don't purge what they eat, they tend to be quite overweight, even though they may diet or exercise or try other ways to control their weight.

However, compulsive overeating should not be confused with being fat. While most compulsive eaters are fat, or even obese, fat people are not necessarily overeaters. In fact, most studies show that fat people do not eat more or that much differently than people who are thinner. Some studies even show that fat people eat *less* than their thin counterparts. That is because our natural weight range and body shape are determined primarily by genetics. Twins who are separated at birth and raised in different environments with very different eating patterns usually remain within only a few pounds of each other's weight.

Here are some common signs of compulsive overeating to look for:

■ Episodes of binge eating, that is, eating rapidly an amount of food that is larger than what most people would eat under similar circumstances

■ Eating when not physically hungry

■ Frequent attempts to control body weight by dieting

■ Feeling out of control when eating and unable to stop

■ Snacking and nibbling over several hours

■ Binge eating generally done in private

■ Preference for high-fat, high-sugar "comfort foods"

■ Eating to relieve stress or unpleasant feelings

■ Feeling depressed and ashamed after binging

■ Restriction of activities or social events because of embarrassment about weight

Compulsive overeating can also be recognized by some of its harmful physical effects:

■ Weight gain, sometimes to the point of obesity

■ Weight-related hypertension or fatigue

■ Increased risk of high blood pressure, clogged blood vessels, heart attack, stroke, certain cancers, and diabetes

■ Increased risk of bone and joint problems

If you are a compulsive overeater, you need to be very concerned about the long-term harmful effects the disorder can have on you.

Are You an Overeater?

Mary, age 16, grew up very heavy. By the time she entered the seventh grade, she weighed close to 180 pounds. That's when she went on her first diet. She lost 40 pounds, but she became so obsessed with food—either eating or not eating—that each day became a struggle for her.

She gained back much of the weight that she had lost, going from 140 pounds in eighth grade to 165 pounds in her sophomore year in high school. "By far the most important event in my day was mealtime. I used food for nearly every purpose—to pep me up, slow me down, or calm tension. When I felt like wallowing in self-pity, I turned to food."

Every day after school, when she got home, she had to fight a battle of willpower against food. "I usually had to have something to eat by four o'clock—or, who knows, I might faint. After all, six o'clock was so far away, and I needed a fix. I suffered from cramps, indigestion, and constipation. My family was extremely concerned about my obsession."

When Mary got her driver's license in the spring of her sophomore year, she began going to meetings of Overeaters Anonymous (OA). With their help she began the process of recovering from her disorder.

The Overeaters Anonymous Quiz
Overeaters Anonymous (OA) has a quiz for teenagers who think they have a problem. Take it and see how you do.

Weight gain may occur when people become less active, but for teens, who are already very active, the cause is usually emotional.

■ Do you eat as a response to all kinds of feelings—highs, lows, and in-betweens?

■ Does your overeating make you miserable?

■ Do you eat normally in front of others and binge when you're alone?

■ Do you hate gym and other activities because you are embarrassed about your weight?

■ Do you spend more money than you would like to on junk food?

■ Do you sometimes steal food—or money to buy it?

■ Do you pass up dances and other events because you can't fit into nice clothes?

■ Do you resent people's comments and "helpful suggestions" about your weight or the amount of food you eat?

If you answered yes to most of the questions, you suffer from a compulsive overeating disorder. But you are not alone. The illness afflicts many teenagers—both male and female—as well as many older adults.

How Compulsive Eating Develops

Compulsive overeating begins more gradually than anorexia and bulimia. Often it begins in early childhood and is shaped by family eating patterns. Did your family use food to feel good, fill up empty time, or avoid feelings? Did your parents show you by their example that the best way to deal with emotions is to eat?

Although overeating may not cause you to put on that much weight while you are growing and active, weight problems will develop when you stop growing or become less active.

Adolescent Changes
Your teen years may be the most difficult and confusing time you will ever face. In a few short years, you experience tremendous physical, social, and emotional changes, including changes in your relationships with your family, friends, and members of the opposite sex. While all these changes are a normal part of growing up, some adolescents feel overwhelmed and may turn to food to help them cope with their problems.

Family Patterns
Compulsive overeating often runs in families. Most overeaters come from families that overemphasize food, make it abundantly available, and focus on how much people eat. One compulsive overeater said, "In my family, how much you liked my mother's cooking was measured by how much you ate. It didn't matter whether or not you were hungry. Making my mother feel good was what counted." Unlike the case with anorexics and bulimics, a high proportion of compulsive overeaters are male.

Compulsive overeaters usually eat in binges and, unlike bulimics, take steps short of purging, like dieting or exercising, to try to lose the weight they gain. Some authorities in the field of eating disorders now designate binge eating disorder (without the purging) as a separate illness to differentiate it from the binge/purge cycle that characterizes bulimia.

Emotional Roots of Compulsive Eating

Chronic overeating can be a lifelong problem fueled by poor dietary habits and serious psychological and physical problems. Like the bulimic, the compulsive overeater will try

Common Symptoms of Eating Disorders

Symptoms	Anorexia Nervosa*	Bulimia Nervosa*	Binge Eating Disorder
Excessive weight loss in relatively short period of time	■		
Continuation of dieting although bone-thin	■		
Dissatisfaction with appearance; belief that body is fat, even though severely underweight	■		
Loss of monthly menstrual periods	■	■	
Unusual interest in food and development of strange eating rituals	■	■	
Eating in secret	■	■	■
Obsession with exercise	■	■	
Serious depression	■	■	■
Binging—consumption of large amounts of food		■	■
Vomiting or use of drugs to stimulate vomiting, bowel movements, and urination		■	
Binging but no noticeable weight gain		■	
Disappearance into bathroom for long periods of time to induce vomiting		■	
Abuse of drugs or alcohol		■	■

*Some individuals suffer from anorexia and bulimia and have symptoms of both disorders.
Source: National Institute of Health

everything he can to stop eating. He will fast or go on a rigid diet, but inevitably the diet collapses. The next binge overtakes him, and he feels lost.

Diets Don't Work
Diets and weight reduction programs may help in the short run, but they are not a solution in the long run because they don't deal with the emotional roots of overeating. In fact, strict diets are harmful because they only set the stage for the next overeating binge. Denying your body the food it needs only creates a strong craving that your body needs to satisfy by eating. This cycle of binging and dieting can go on indefinitely.

Overeating Is Misunderstood
Unfortunately, the emotional roots of compulsive overeating are not taken seriously enough. Too many people blame overeaters for their problem by labeling them as lazy, gluttonous, or lacking in self-control. Instead of being addressed as a disorder having psychological causes, overeating is treated simply as a matter of food, diet, and weight. This neglect of the emotional roots of the problem can keep the binging episodes going for years. Only when the emotional factors are considered—as well as the question of a healthy diet—can the problem be dealt with.

CHAPTER 6

Confronting the Problem

Q Claudia used to be my best friend, but we aren't that close anymore. She keeps to herself mostly, and I have other friends and a boyfriend, too. Something's definitely wrong with Claudia. She's all skin and bones. It's scary. I feel a little guilty because we used to be such good friends. Should I try to do something to help her?

A Your friend Claudia is in trouble, and you're right to be concerned. That she is "skin and bones" and keeps to herself more than she used to is a warning signal. She's probably anorexic. Her thinness and isolation are definitely signs that something's seriously wrong, and you need to get involved as soon as you can.

• • • • • • • • • • • •

Show That You Care
You need to talk to Claudia about your concern. You may need to talk to her parents or the guidance counselor at school, as well. They may already be aware of the problem, but showing your concern will not hurt.

Claudia may be feeling inadequate and depressed. Perhaps your success at winning new friends and having a boyfriend is making her feel left out or left behind. As is the case with all eating disorders, the real problem has to do with what's going on inside.

She probably would like you to reach out to her and show that you still care even though you've grown apart. Make an extra effort to talk to her. Find out what's going on and tell her about your concern.

Whether your friend or you are the one with the disorder, try to act as soon as possible. Eating disorders do not get better by themselves. Untreated, they will only get worse and lead to further unhappiness, serious illness, hospitalization, and sometimes even death. The longer eating disorders are allowed to continue, the harder they are to treat.

Prevention

Obviously, the best way to avoid an eating disorder is to prevent it from developing in the first place. Now that you know what eating disorders are and have a better idea of how serious they can be, you should know about steps to take to prevent an eating disorder from developing:

■ Look out for the warning signs of an eating disorder and make informed choices about ways to avoid the problem.

■ Don't hang around with other teens who obsess about food, dieting, and weight, or who binge, purge, or starve themselves.

■ Don't judge yourself by the standard of how people look in fashion magazines, movies, or on TV.

■ Don't get a job in a food-related business if you think it could cause you to develop an obsession with food.

■ Don't keep a scale in your room or bathroom or any other place where you can get to it easily.

■ Don't eat when you're not hungry, and don't let anybody make you eat.

■ Learn to speak up when something's on your mind, so that you won't always be tempted to use food as a substitute for communicating with others.

■ Engage in activities and develop skills that will help you improve your self-confidence, sense of control, and ability to communicate.

Self-awareness

The first step in fighting an emerging eating disorder is to admit having a problem. Being honest about it is the best way to keep it from getting worse. Self-awareness will help you get a handle on your eating disorder and keep it from getting a handle on you.

When Do You Binge?
If you're the one with the problem, one thing you can do is identify the times of the day when you're most likely to give in to a binge or to restrict what you eat. Think also about the kind of foods you are most likely to binge on. That will help you to control what you buy when it comes time for a binge.

What Sets You Off?
Be aware of negative triggers that upset you and make you want to binge. Learn to speak up about them. For example, if your mother keeps saying something that gets you upset and drives you to the refrigerator, tell her so.

Keeping a log may help you become more aware of your eating habits; to try this approach, get a notebook and keep a record of what you eat and when. Keep special track of the times when you binge. What were you feeling? What triggered the binge? What did you eat and how much? Self-awareness is the key to controlling your eating problem instead of letting it control you.

Talk to Somebody

As we discussed in Chapter 1, talking to somebody about your problem is the first step to coming to terms with it. And the sooner, the better. Most teens who suffer from eating disorders do so in secret, so breaking the silence can be very difficult. But talking to somebody about your eating disorder is absolutely essential to recovery.

Eating Disorders Reflect Emotional Disorders

Some teens with eating disorders use their worry about weight or body shape as a way to focus on what's outside rather than inside. For example, if an anorexic teen seems to be worried about "Am I thin enough?" she is probably really worried about "Am I good enough?" Many teens focus on body shape as a way to convert their concern about what's inside into a concern about what is really going on outside.

Eating disorders do not usually show up in teens who are emotionally healthy, active, involved, and generally satisfied with their lives. Teens with eating disorders are those who have chosen this destructive way to feel better about themselves and to cope with their troubled world as best they can.

Good friends can help each other confront problems. If you suspect a friend has an eating disorder, talk to him or her about it. If you're the one with the problem, don't keep it to yourself.

Escape Through Eating

An eating disorder can function as a form of substance abuse, like drinking or taking drugs. When used for emotional purposes, food can function like a drug or alcohol by providing an escape. Many teens with eating disorders also struggle with low energy levels and feelings of sadness and hopelessness.

An eating disorder can also be a way to numb unpleasant feelings. Teens with eating disorders often have trouble acknowledging, accepting, and experiencing their feelings. They may be afraid of being overwhelmed by strong feelings or of overwhelming others with them. Fear of strong emotions can drive a teen to food. Teens with eating disorders tend to keep many of their feelings and desires secret—sometimes even secret from themselves.

How to Help Somebody Else

Let's return to your friend, Claudia. Some teens with eating disorders cannot or will not seek help by themselves. They may not even think they have a problem. Or, they may know something's wrong, but don't want to talk about it or don't know how to go about it. In those cases *the teen with the problem needs to be spoken to.*

Eating disorders are too dangerous to ignore. So, if you're really concerned about Claudia, find a way to approach her so that you bring your concern to her attention.

Here are some specific things you can do:

■ Prepare to talk to Claudia by finding out all you can about eating disorders by reading this book and any other reading material you can find. If possible, talk to a therapist or doctor in your community who treats eating disorders.

■ Begin your talk with Claudia by letting her know you care and are concerned about what is happening to her.

■ Keep the focus on the behavior you observe—eating junk food, sudden weight loss due to intense dieting, obsession with calories and body shape, binge eating, and skipping meals. Ask Claudia if something is bothering her, and ask if there is something you can do to help.

■ Be prepared for denial. Many teens with eating problems refuse to admit they have a problem, even to themselves. Claudia may get defensive and say there's nothing wrong. She may even get angry and tell you to mind your own business. Don't take it personally. Don't be put off or get angry back. Your friend needs you. Tell her you are only talking to her because you care and want to help.

If the conversation ends badly, with Claudia getting angry and defensive, don't worry. You have done what you needed to do, and both your words and your concern will make a difference. Later she may admit she has a problem and may be willing to talk more about it. She may even ask you for help. Feel good that you took the initiative. Claudia will appreciate your efforts on her behalf and someday may even thank you.

CHAPTER 7

Treatment

Q I've been dieting for over a year now, but the more I diet, the more I seem to need to. I keep telling myself I'm doing it because I want to, but I know that's not true. Dieting has taken over my life. I met a girl at school who says she had the same problem. She goes to a therapist. Sometimes I think maybe I should, too. Should I?

A Good for you for realizing you can't solve your problem by yourself. By admitting you can't go it alone any-more—and don't want to—you're taking an important step toward recovery.

• • • • • • • • • • • •

Experts on eating disorders agree that the most effective and long-lasting treatment for an eating disorder is some form of psychotherapy. This is a big step for you to think about taking, but the fact that you're willing to consider it is a very positive sign. It shows that *you* want to take control of your life, rather than allowing your eating problem to remain in control.

Available Treatments

For teens with eating disorders, there are several kinds of treatment available. These include psychotherapy (individual, family, and group), support and self-help groups, medical treatment, nutritional counseling, medication, and, in the most extreme cases, hospitalization. The best treatment for you will be one that is tailored to you as an individual—to your special problems, needs, and strengths, as well as to the nature and severity of your disorder. You need to find the treatment that will be most effective for you.

What Is Therapy?

The most effective treatment for an eating disorder is some form of psychotherapy (most often called simply "therapy"). You may not know what psychotherapy is exactly or what you can expect from it. When some people hear the term "therapy," they immediately think "shrink." They may believe that going into therapy means having a psychiatrist dictate to them what they should think and how they should act, but that is not an accurate picture.

Therapy Is a Partnership
Good therapy is a partnership between you and your therapist. Your therapist may be a trained social worker, a psychologist, or a psychiatrist who in his or her capacity as a medical doctor is licensed to prescribe medication.

Therapy is a two-way street: the therapist listens to you and makes suggestions about how you can improve things in your life. You listen to the therapist and respond to those suggestions that feel right to you. The two of you *together* come to an understanding of your situation and what's best for you. This can be an uncomfortable process sometimes if what the therapist has to say isn't what you want to hear. However, like any two-way communication, it gives you the chance to grow.

Individual, Family, and Group Therapy
Therapy that is one-on-one is called individual therapy. When family members take part in the discussions with you and the therapist, that is called family therapy. When several people

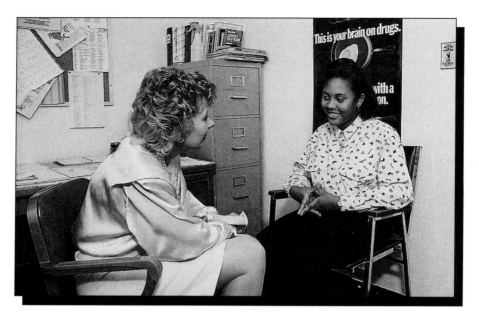

Working with a therapist can help a person work through emotional problems and succeed in overcoming an eating disorder.

who are seeing the same therapist meet together with the therapist to discuss their problems, that is called group therapy.

Whatever the form of the therapy, it needs to address both the symptoms of the eating disorder and the underlying psychological factors. Exclusive attention to either the symptoms or the underlying causes may impede and prolong the recovery process.

Individual psychotherapy. In individual therapy you meet with your therapist alone at least once a week, with each session lasting about 45 minutes. While the therapy will deal with the visible symptoms of binging, purging, or self-starvation, it will also address the psychological factors under the surface of the disorder. The goal of the treatment will be not only to stop the behavior, but also to have you understand exactly how and why you are using food as a response to your emotional needs.

Family therapy. In family therapy, sessions involve not just you but members of your family as well. They may include parents, siblings, or any other relatives living with you. In family therapy, an eating disorder is usually seen as a sign of trouble in the family as a whole, not just with the person who has the eating disorder. Family problems may include difficulties between the parents, family rules that suppress feelings, lack of honest communication, or even just the inability to enjoy and appreciate each other. Family problems are discussed by all the family members, and everybody is encouraged to change, not just the person with the eating disorder.

Group therapy. A group usually consists of five to twelve people who meet with a therapist once a week. Some groups focus specifically on eating issues, while others address a wider range of emotional problems. Group therapy helps counter feelings of being all alone with your problem. As you try to change your eating habits, a group can help you with encouragement and support. It can also be a place to learn how to improve your ability to express your feelings and to trust and interact with others.

Support and Self-help Groups

Whether you are presently in therapy for your eating disorder or not, support groups offer a good way to get help for your problem. These groups consist of people at various stages of crisis or recovery who meet to share their experiences. The terms "support groups" and "self-help groups" are used interchangeably; however, self-help groups usually have no professional facilitator, whereas support groups usually are led by a trained person. While these groups are where some people start their recovery, they are not meant to be a substitute for psychotherapy. For many people, self-help groups are only a first step toward realizing they are not alone and that recovery is possible.

Support and self-help groups can meet anywhere from daily to once a month. As their name suggests, they are not psychotherapy groups run by a therapist. If a therapist attends, he or she remains in the background. The person who leads the meeting is usually somebody who has recovered from an eating disorder and thus can use his or her experience as a source of inspiration and guidance.

Self-help groups are inexpensive. Because they do not employ the services of a trained professional, they usually are free or merely charge a nominal fee to pay for the meeting space. Meetings can be attended as needed; participants do not have to commit themselves to the group. Since people are free to come and go, membership can change from meeting to meeting. Some groups publish their own newsletters and hold monthly meetings with speakers.

Support group meetings vary in how they are organized. Some have no specific agenda, while others have a particular topic that is discussed at each meeting. Some groups start with a speaker and then break up into small groups where participants can share their feelings about the subject discussed.

Medical Treatment

Eating disorders require a thorough medical evaluation before treatment can begin. The damage that disordered eating does to the body requires the attention of such specialists as internists, dentists, gynecologists, and nutritionists. When you go to a therapist for a consultation about your eating problem, the therapist may recommend an examination by one or more of these specialists.

As we stated earlier, there are numerous medical complications that result from damage done by disordered eating. For example, a bulimic who has been vomiting up her food needs to see a dentist, since bulimics are susceptible to tooth decay as a result of enamel erosion from regurgitated stomach acids. With both anorexia and bulimia, a gynecologist is needed to examine changes in the menstrual cycle caused by weight fluctuations and poor nutrition.

Nutrition

Therapy for an eating disorder should also include consultations with a nutritionist. Teens with eating disorders have extremely irregular eating patterns. Many of them may not have had a normal meal in months or even years. That's where nutritionists come in. They're trained to correct nutritional imbalances and plan healthy diet programs. They can provide you with accurate information about food and diet and can also help you to devise meal plans and eating strategies that will help you get control of your food-related obsessions and compulsions.

Medication

In some cases, a therapist may request that a psychiatrist who specializes in eating disorders meet with the patient to evaluate the advisability of medication. Much research is now being done on the effectiveness of medication on the suppression of eating disorder behaviors. So far there is little evidence that medication can help anorexics and compulsive overeaters, but there is some preliminary evidence that antidepressants may help some bulimics reduce their binging and purging.

Hospitalization

Hospitalization is highly recommended when an eating disorder has led to either physical problems that are life-threatening or to severe psychological or behavioral dysfunction.

Treatment for an eating disorder can be long and costly, and is not always successful. In those cases, the disorder continues despite treatment, or the physical or psychological damage is so extensive that it leads to death. For treatment to be successful, it needs to begin as early as possible.

Choosing a Therapist

When you consider selecting a therapist, you should begin by thinking about your preferences. For example, would you prefer to have a male therapist or a female therapist? Does the age of the therapist make any difference to you? These are questions to consider as you go about selecting a therapist.

Once you or your parents have acquired the name of one or more therapists, you should make an appointment for a consultation. The therapist will listen to what you have to say and give you his or her opinion about the best way to approach the problem. That is the best time to ask questions that will help you decide if you want to work with the therapist:

■ Ask about credentials and experience. Is the therapist licensed or in the process of being licensed? Does the therapist have experience treating eating disorders or other obsessive-compulsive disorders?

■ How much will the treatment cost?

■ Find out the therapist's policy regarding parental involvement. Will the therapist be talking to your parents? If so, how much and under what conditions? If there is a serious problem or crisis, will the therapist inform your parents?

■ Will medication ever be used? If so, when and under what conditions?

■ Will other therapies—group or family—be used along with individual therapy?

Consulting with more than one therapist will give you a feeling for how different people work. You should feel comfortable with the person with whom you will be working. A good bond with your therapist will help you through difficult times and make your treatment all the more effective.

Reach Out for Help

Whether you're the teen with the eating problem yourself or you're a teen trying to help somebody else, it is important to remember that there are people around who care and are willing to get involved and help if you ask them. But they have to know something's wrong before they can offer their help. So, if you have an eating disorder or know somebody who does, break the silence and reach out for help. You'll be glad you did.

Where to Go for Help

Your school probably has a guidance counselor or somebody else who can give you advice and help you find a doctor or therapist with training and experience with eating disorders.

You can also ask your local hospital or university medical center for the location of the eating disorder clinic nearest you.

Listed below are several national organizations that will be glad to answer your questions.

About Face—Anorexia and
   Bulimia Outreach Facilities
1393 Avenue Road
Toronto, ON M5N 2H3

American Anorexia/Bulimia
   Association (AABA)
425 East 61st Street, 6th Floor
New York, NY 10021
(212) 891-8686

Anorexia Bulimia Care (ABC)
545 Concord Avenue
Cambridge, MA 02138-1122
(617) 492-7670

Anorexia Nervosa and Related
   Eating Disorders (ANRED)
P.O. Box 5112
Eugene, OR 97405
(503) 344-1144

Center for the Study of
   Anorexia and Bulimia
1 West 91st Street
New York, NY 10024
(212) 595-3449

Eating Disorders Awareness
   & Prevention (EDAP)
255 Alhambra Circle, #321
Coral Gables, FL 33134
(305) 444-3731

Foundation for Education about
   Eating Disorders (FEED)
5238 Duvall Drive
Bethesda, MD 20816

International Association of
   Eating Disorders
   Professionals (IAEDP)
123 NW 13th Street, #206
Boca Raton, FL 33432-1618
(407) 338-6494

Kids Help Phone
2 Bloor Street West, #100
P.O. Box 513
Toronto, ON M4W 3E2
(800) 668-6868

National Association of
   Anorexia Nervosa and
   Associated Disorders
   (ANAD)
P.O. Box 7
Highland Park, IL 60035
(708) 831-3438

National Association to Advance
   Fat Acceptance (NAAFA)
P.O. Box 188620
Sacramento, CA 95818
(916) 558-6880

Where to Go for Help

National Eating Disorders
   Information Centre (NEDIC)
Women's College Hospital
College Wing 1-304
200 Elizabeth Street
Toronto, ON M56 2C4
(416) 340-4156

National Eating Disorders
   Organization (NEDO)
[formerly National Anorexic
   Aid Society (NAAS)]
445 East Granville Road
Worthington, OH 43085
(614) 436-1112

Overeaters Anonymous (OA)
World Services Office
383 Van Ness Avenue, Suite
   1601
Torrance, CA 90501
Mailing Address:
P.O. Box 92870
Los Angeles, CA 90009
(310) 618-8835

For More Information

Books

An asterisk (*) indicates a young adult book.

Boskind-White, Marlene, and William C. White, Jr. *Bulimarexia: The Binge/Purge Cycle* (2nd ed.). Norton, 1991.

Bruch, Hilde. *The Golden Cage: The Enigma of Anorexia Nervosa.* Vintage, 1979.

Chernin, Kim. *The Obsession: Reflections on the Tyranny of Slenderness.* Harper & Row, 1981.

Hall, Lindsey, and Leigh Cohn. *Bulimia: A Guide to Recovery.* Gurze, 1992.

Hirschmann, Jane, and Carol Munter. *Overcoming Overeating.* Addison-Wesley, 1988.

Hirschmann, Jane, and Lela Zaphiropolous. *Preventing Childhood Eating Problems.* Gurze, 1993.

Kano, Susan. *Making Peace with Food: Freeing Yourself from the Diet-Weight Obsession* (rev. ed.). HarperCollins, 1989.

* Kolodny, Nancy. *When Food's a Foe: How to Confront and Conquer Eating Disorders.* Little, Brown, 1992.

* Kubersky, Rachel. *Everything You Need to Know about Eating Disorders.* Rosen, 1992.

* Landau, Elaine. *Why Are They Starving Themselves?* Julian Messner, 1983.

For More Information

Levenkron, Steven. *The Best Little Girl in the World*. Warner, 1979.

Levine, Michael, and Laura Hill. *A 5-Day Lesson Plan on Eating Disorders: Grades 7–12*. National Eating Disorders Organization (NEDO), 1991.

* Maloney, Michael, and Rachel Kranz. *Straight Talk About Eating Disorders*. Facts On File, 1991.

* Moe, Barbara. *Coping with Eating Disorders*. Rosen, 1991.

* Nardo, Don. *Eating Disorders*. Lucent, 1991.

O'Neill, Cherry Boone. *Starving for Attention: A Young Woman's Struggle and Triumph over Anorexia Nervosa*. LifeCares, 1992.

Roth, Geneen. *Feeding the Hungry Heart: The Experience of Compulsive Eating*. Signet, 1983.

Roth, Geneen. *When Food Is Love*. New American Library, 1993.

Schroeder, Charles. *Fat Is Not a Four-Letter Word*. Chronimed, 1992.

Siegel, Michele, et al. *Surviving an Eating Disorder: New Perspectives and Strategies for Family and Friends*. Harper & Row, 1988.

* Sonder, Ben. *Eating Disorders: When Food Turns Against You*. Franklin Watts, 1993.

Videotapes

Faces of Recovery (35 min.) [aka *Cathy Rigby on Eating Disorders*]. *In Our Own Words: Personal Accounts of Eating Disorders* (50 min.). Contact: Gurze Books, P.O. Box 2238, Carlsbad, CA 92018, (800) 756-7533.

Skin Deep: A Story About Eating Disorder Prevention (26 min., for grades 7-12). Contact: Coronet/MTI Film & Video, 108 Wilmot Road, Deerfield, IL 60015, (800) 777-2400.

Wasting Away: Understanding Anorexia Nervosa and Bulimia (40 min.).

You Can Be Too Thin: Understanding Anorexia and Bulimia (57 min.). Contact: Guidance Associates, P.O. Box 1000, Mount Kisco, NY 10549-0010, (800) 431-1242 or (914) 666-4100.

Audiocassettes

Breaking Free (Geneen Roth's workshop—4 cassettes).

Overcoming Overeating, by Jane Hirschmann and Carol Munter (4 cassettes).

Understanding Bulimia, by Lindsey Hall and Leigh Cohn (55 min.). Contact: Gurze Books, P.O. Box 2238, Carlsbad, CA 92018, (800) 756-7533.

INDEX